Praise for Dreaming of the Rain in Brooklyn

"*Dreaming of the Rain in Brooklyn* marks the debut of a poet of deep feeling, one who filters the 'pear light of hope' through daily existence and who recognizes each 'odd hour... pressed by love.' In poems resplendent with 'creation's frenzy,' with jazz, lovers, and 'Noah's lucky ones,' those creatures great and small, Howard Faerstein acknowledges a world, past and present, that remains 'wonderful even with death.'"
—Michael Waters, author of *Gospel Night*

"Earthy and savvy, hungry and rueful, Howard Faerstein's poems have an ear for the vernacular and an eye for the unsolvable. His offbeat America, from Brooklyn to the Southwest, is a place of ruin and hope, as full of heart and surprise as a jazz solo. He takes us to 'all the bad parts of town,' where the enduring itches of body and soul keep finding their way into fresh song."
—Joan Larkin, author of *My Body: New and Selected Poems*

DREAMING OF THE RAIN IN BROOKLYN

Dreaming of the Rain in Brooklyn

Poems

Howard Faerstein

Press 53

Winston-Salem

Press 53, LLC
PO Box 30314
Winston-Salem, NC 27130

First Edition

Silver Concho Poetry Series

Cover design by Kevin Morgan Watson

Cover art, "Rain," Copyright © 2013 by Matthew Priestley,
used by permission of the artist.
Matthew Priestley Photography Ltd ABIPP
www.mattpriestley.co.uk

Author photo by Claire Lamberg

Printed on acid-free paper
ISBN 978-1-935708-77-3

For Jan, for keeps

Acknowledgments

The author wishes to thank the editors of the following journals in which these poems first appeared:

5 A.M., "My New House"

The Berkshire Review, "Taking a Chance on Love," "The Sound in the Middle of 'Moon'"

Central Avenue, "Saturday Night in Arroyo Seco, Abe's Bar & Grill"

Common Ground Review, "Longing," "Baby in the Boat"

Comstock Review, "When Dexter Gordon and Freddie Hubbard Play *I'm a Fool to Love You*"

Connotation Press: An Online Artifact, "Hunger," "Paradise Alley," "People Next Door"

Cutthroat, a Journal of the Arts, "Russian Wood," "The Machine," "Crossfire," "The Flamingo's Tongue," "The Enticement of St. Anthony," "In Great Expectation," "Doo Wop for Fidel," "Birding Mount Auburn Cemetery, Cambridge," "In Reply To," "The Extinction of the Black Rhino in our Time"

Diner, "The First Time I Saw the World"

Dirty Napkin, "Talk of Sports and Youth Turns to Sex and Mourning"

Downtown Brooklyn, "I Go Back as Far as Brooklyn"

Equinox, "I Knew When I Saw this Place"

Great River Review, "In the Narrows"

Gris-Gris, "Mid-Autumn's Eve," "The Difference between Two Readings"

Main Street Rag, "Ungano's"

Manzanita Quarterly, "A Song for Clifford"

Meat for Tea, "Or Did I"

Mudfish, "1000 Islands"

Naugatuck Review, "One Day at the Junction," "Beds and Sinks"

Nimrod, "Missionary Ridge"

The November 3rd Club, "Draft Induction Day, 1969"

The Prairie Star, "Hairpin Turn"

Silkworm, "Anonymous Love—Cecropia"

Tygerburning, "Wasn't That a Boy"

Dreaming of the Rain in Brooklyn

Taking a Chance on Love   xv

I

The First Time I Saw the World   3
I Go Back as Far as Brooklyn   4
Beds and Sinks   5
Draft Induction Day, 1969   6
Paradise Alley   7
Longing   11
Wasn't That a Boy   12
Or Did I   13
Ungano's   15
Missionary Ridge   16
The Sound in the Middle of "Moon"   18
Russian Wood   19
Inside Out   20
Four Years in Sandisfield   21
Looking for the East Meadows   22
Mid-Autumn's Eve   23
I Knew When I Saw This Place It Would Hold   24
Hairpin Turn   25

II

I Can't Help Myself   29
In the Narrows   30
Baby in the Boat   31
Meditation on a Dream Unrecalled   32
Incident at the Baggage Carousel   33
People Next Door   35
Not Always Wishing for Truth   38
In Reply To   40
Hunger   41
Saturday Night in Arroyo Seco, Abe's Bar & Grill   43
My New House   44

Crossfire   45
After Driving Through El Duende, New Mexico   46
A Song for Clifford   47
A Song for Jack   48
Lucky to Have   50
Reentry   51
Still Life with Self-Portrait   52

III

Doo Wop for Fidel   57
The Flamingo's Tongue   59
Even the Dog Took on Vulnerability   62
The Enticement of St. Anthony   63
One Day at the Junction   64
The Machine   65
1000 Islands   66
New Moon—Memorial for a Colleague   67
When Dexter Gordon and Freddie Hubbard
    Play *I'm a Fool to Want You*   70
Talk of Sports and Youth Turns to Sex and Mourning 71
Kindling   72
Anonymous Love: Cecropia   73
Horse Story   74
Before It Ended   75
Birding Mount Auburn Cemetery, Cambridge   76
Carolina Wren   77
The Extinction of the Black Rhino in Our Time, or
    Older Man Emerging from Flowers   79
The Difference between Two Readings   81
In Great Expectation   82

Taking a Chance on Love

Man, I was riffing today
—Louis Armstrong

I don't want you taken in.

I don't want to take it or leave it.

I don't want you to take me lightly.

I want to take you for a ride through the Lower East Side.

To a ballgame in Fenway and later that night Madison Square,

        then for hotcakes in a diner in San Rafael.

I want to take you seriously.

I want you to take me to heart.

I want to take you where mountain laurel blooms,

        monarchs gather, bats dart.

I want to take you on the B65 downtown bus, get off on Gates,

        turn down Fulton.

I want to take you to Notre Dame's lost and found.

To a minimalist exhibit in a maximum museum.

I want you to take it to the bank.

I don't want you to take my word for it.

I want to take you in the market at St. Jean de Luz.

In Quaker Cemetery in Prospect Park.

In Momo Taro, Noguchi's egg high on a hill.

I don't want to be taken to the cleaners.

I never want to take you for granted.

I want to take you to La Jolla tide pools.

All the places we've never been.

All the bad parts of town.

I

The First Time I Saw the World

I was happy.
It's been wonderful even with death.
Tripping each night over a different limb,
beech birch balsam,
inventing love along the blind road.

Nothing has stopped me.
Down the same steps every evening.
Redwings flying through late March snow.
Make a sound like Lear in a storm.
Do not abdicate.

I want to tell everything.
How I crave cake but rarely eat it.
About my aunt living in a schoolroom
and my uncle bathing in limes.
How as a child I asked,

Why do we all think different if we're all the same
teeth arms feet?

Trees stretching in warmth,
nighthawks in hidden sky.
You're not home from high school,
stoned, when your mom opens the door.
You're old, the age of beheading,

fixed still by symmetry,
lemony light of regret,
pear light of hope.
Each dusk footfalls in black wind.
Dirt dragged through the small hours.

Moon mouthing
Do not forget me.

I Go Back as Far as Brooklyn

I go back as far as Brooklyn and its dark brown trees,
forsythia, too, inside fenced curbside plots
fronting bars & beauty parlors, the long avenues
pop-ups from picture books,
and everything a puzzle waiting to be solved
like sycamore bark & the building courtyard
crowded with Catholic girls in Easter outfits.

It was the time of the Cold War.
My transistor radio was subverted by race music.
On my knees I prayed my parents would vanish
behind an iron curtain or disappear under the boardwalk.
I had no dog to run alongside me when bike riding
past the wide plane trees I loved so much & left far behind
in that city of buses & cabs when I was small.

Beds and Sinks

In the supermart the young mother
leaning into her cart,
filling the counter with formula and fennel seed,
coriander and face cream,
has a love bite on her left breast,
and those in line, staring,
motionless, remember...

The argument between staying and going.
The irreconcilable dilemma of connection and solitude.
All the loving on unmade dented beds.
The sourness amid the giggling during Friday assembly.
And all the sinks we've washed in, the dishes.
All the dining room tables bought and sold.
And the pull between meadow and garden.
And children lifted high
in the face of implacable crows, indifferent kingfishers.
And all the clapping and weeping.
All the blue stones and the bay's whelk shells.
And the transpiration inside the tree nursery:

This is because of the laughter and the breathing we do.

Draft Induction Day, 1969

Because I had no plan to run for President
& was not yet a felon
I walked into Fort Hamilton armed
with drugs & a therapist's letter.

Ed was there, scratching his thighs furiously,
blood pooling beneath the legs of the stool
& I watched Johnny strip down,
peanut butter spread about his cheeks,
even in the valley of his hole.

I failed the physical's every test
& by the end how exhausted I was
by the boys waiting to kill, longing to die,
gathered around to copy my answers even as I told them
every one was wrong.

Then the news I was "fit as a fiddle"
but had to return next morning to see the shrink.
Nothing of what I recounted made a bit of difference—
homo, junkie, opposed to the imperial conflict—
but when I explained how I cured myself of syphillis
while living in a California commune
by cutting the tip of my penis into four symmetrical parts
he hesitated then said *It's against my better judgement but I'm giving you*

I leaped off the chair in great joy,
grabbing the paper,
  a 4F
& headed for the discharge desk where I was jeered & scowled at
& hand-in-hand with Johnny
I skipped out on the pavement of Shore Parkway,
scows plying the Narrows,
carriers taking the boys from Sunset Park & Bed-Stuy
to Chu Lai, to Hua Ky.

Paradise Alley

who ate fire in paint hotels or drank turpentine in Paradise Alley
—Allen Ginsberg, "Howl"

In 1968, before the moon landing
& after the Summer of Love,
as a favor I dropped off homemade meth
to a guy whose girlfriend's black hair was streaked with silver.
As soon as he injected a match head's worth
he collapsed
& I was sure he was dead
but when he came to minutes later
he thanked me—
It was the best—
& he wanted more
as if there were any more.

When I thought I'd killed him I was in a sweat.
The girl in the half-plastered brick room
decorated with album covers—
The Fish, The Mothers, The Dead—
was crying.

I had no wisdom whatsoever.
All I wanted was a journey.

~

Billy the Greek told me I had a weak mind
& it was true.
Too weak to sleep only once
with Jeanette, the Barbados woman.
It wasn't long before she hit me with a chair,
startled cats diving for cover
in that ground floor apartment by the park.
A patrol car every night in front.
Her skin browner than oak leaves after frost.

~

I still dream of Nixon resigning & my father,
who kept his autographed picture on an end table,
driving through Brooklyn
picking up shirts and blouses
from the Ebbets Field project
& from the judges on Prospect Park West.
He'd take them to Mel's Dry Cleaners on Greene Street,
pick them up 2 days later,
price & mark them in his store,
then deliver them to the judges & projects.
When I dealt I did the same.
Bought an ounce of hash from Vinnie for $90
sold it to friends for $100.
I'm so like my father,
a middleman running errands

~

He came to my apartment when Jeanette was living there.
Seeing her, he dropped the bundled laundry & fled.

~

On the way back from Paradise Alley
Ian ran a light on Myrtle Avenue.
A beat cop waved us down but Ian floored the Chevy
& the cop commandeered a gypsy cab,
giving chase through the breathless ghetto. We won.
Ian, found dead a week later in his backseat, drove back,
searching for the tossed out drugs.

~

Dock Ellis says he pitched a no-hitter on acid.
In my case, I read *The Times* stock quotes to my father.
It made him happy, he said, for us to be closer.

After the killings at Kent State
all of America went on pass/fail
& so I graduated college.

~

Those who despised the government & its war,
those who hated all authority,
provocateurs, opportunists, pacifists,
those hoping to get laid,
thousands coughed in a fog of pepper spray
in the middle of Connecticut Avenue.

Wex threw a brick at an unmarked car.
Two cops stepped out,
hands on pistols.
From the rooftop came more bricks.
The cops quickly back in their car,
plowing their way around the block.

~

After Janis sang
& the Southern Comfort tossed,
thoroughbreds reared in the paddock
& throngs of youth camped out
in grassy fields by the racetrack parking lot.
At dawn I heard a motor start,
someone asleep in a mummy bag in the van's path,
then a scream which has never faded.

~

I introduced Jeanette to my friends.
She slept with a few & later,
in an armed robbery,
paid a surprise visit on Paul,
clerking the late shift at the 8th Street Bookstore.

~

After fleeing New York
I lived on a cliff,
sun & fire those months of hiding.
No one to visit & the cops didn't know me.
It was so quiet in California
walking on red tide beaches
I could hear stray shells & buried mines
popping in the East.

~

On the night Jeanette & I made up
an astronaut stepped out on the moon.
Looking up, he saw the Earth,
half in shadow,
half light.

Longing

I was 14 when my brother
    took me to hear Charles Mingus forswear the bass
    then debate the jazz priest on the existence of God.

My mother brought me to Ripley's *Believe It Or Not* on 42nd Street
    where lurid circus fleas towing dollhouse furniture
    shared a basement with instruments of torture.

My father drove me to Coney Island and we played skee-ball.

    I want my mother back, smoking at our kitchen table.
        She could finish the stories of her youth in the Springfield bakery
        and after I scream *Shut up already Enough*
        I'll blot her tears with my parched lips.

    I want my brother back on the handball court on Colonial Road
        and after I call *do-over* and finally beat him,
        we'll race to Pop G's,
        order malteds, my treat.

    I want my father back on the 4th Avenue bus.
        Lurching past tenements we'll drink sweet Scandinavian liqueur
        and after I fling the schnapps in his face,
        then tell him the damage wasn't lifelong, I'll embrace him.

I want it all back
because it all was so botched.
But that's longing
and longing isn't love.

Wasn't That a Boy

In mother's heart
desperate for a daughter, I was Helene.
Godmother Goldie dropped off a doll carriage;

no one raised a fuss.
Like Rilke in his dress,
wasn't that a boy?

The uproar sparked by my cross-dressing
would have been stifled
if instead of arch-rival

I was daddy's little girl.
And if I weren't a boy,
that summer afternoon in Brighton's shallows

might have readied me
for the disasters I've so often
carried into love.

Enter a stranger offering instruction in the breast stroke.
Looking back toward my brother,
crabs glistening on black rocks,

I take up position, stomach over his hand,
when fingers squirm over my penis
like a fistful of worms.

Quickly reconsidering, I frog-kick his blubber,
jump off and splash back to the blanket.
There was enough for me to do at eight

like imagining myself a father
without protecting my chastity
while swimming in the Atlantic.

Wasn't that a boy!

Or Did I

Five years old when I tell my parents
I'll marry and raise 20 children.
This spring I'll plant witch hazel
for its winter flower.

People say I want too much and I do—
the big break, a kiss goodnight,
putting the lie to the sixth extinction
with a mountain lion asleep on the woodpile,
black swifts dipping above a box canyon in Ouray.

My husky, swiveling her rump, marks a leafpile.
A dozen turkeys scatter-dash into a hemlock stand.
Mother's sighs still sound. Father's laugh still rankles.

After years of searching I glimpsed a roadrunner,
crested flash of lightning
wheeling through dry leaves. Or did I?

Wedged under a coruscated sky,
I'm expecting moonlight
even as muslin clouds tent over steaming stars—
one more blessing, like fatherhood,
late love, like radiance after eclipse.

If nothing is expected
the poem ends,
more space on the page is all.

But what if I were to say
this morning when I woke
waxwings jeweled every tree.

Would you believe me?

Ungano's

Manhattan disco
where Paul J & young transvestites tricked
randy college boys long before *Last Dance*
went gold.

One summer night,
I strode home from the distant shore
& fell through a mirage:
a mini-skirted beauty on 3rd Avenue,
beckoning in such a come-hither way
I could have done it on the sidewalk
fronting Bittar's Pharmacy,
but kissing me so sweetly
was Paul in drag,
whispering...

After Ungano's
I saw him last on *Lifestyles of the Rich and Famous*.
He'd perfected his opulent smile.
Platinum covered the walls.
Obit catalogued his Oscar, #1hits, AIDS,
but not RKO Dyker Saturday matinees,
schoolboys stomping him into sticky aisles.

He was too ballsy to be a woman,
too pretty to be my man.

Missionary Ridge

On October Sundays
when we lived in Colorado
we'd drive to watch the osprey

in Vallecito,
to see if they'd left.
We'd pass the ridge

burned 2 years before,
buffalo & grama grass
rising toward somber foothills.

Under a Neanderthal moon
blackened pine lined the lake's rim
& the raptors flew on

both sides of the darkening road.
We weren't there for the fire,
we were in New Mexico

with its orange-furred bumblebees
& ring-tailed cats
in the ruthless Sandias.

It was a roaming time, my late 50s,
I was always thinking of other towns—
of Roanoke, its crepe myrtles

& I'd begun dreaming of the rain in Brooklyn
& the Italians
wrapping their fig trees in burlap

& a doctor at my daughter's birth
diagnosing an enzyme deficiency
he said would lead to retardation.

He was wrong,
but we spent a day in Bellevue
finding that out in a closet-sized room

filled with broken parents.
Months before Vallecito,
in the dining hall

by the Contoocook,
a phoebe flapped in panic
below the ceiling.

Its mate in a willow outside a window.
In the wildfire
the ospreys stayed with their chicks

as flames slapped at their tree.
I saw the charred
wingtips. Then

talons-first
they plunged
into water.

The Sound in the Middle of "Moon"

Two o's make the sound of taproot,
Owl's hoot, stormtrooper's boot,
Bulletproof.

Two o's make an *oo* like blood.
I've stocked up on things you might want,
Thinking you'd show up or if there was a flood.

Two o's make an *oo* as in buttonwood.
It's understood. As in motherhood.
Like no good.

      You think you know but you don't.

Two o's make the sound of floor.
Morning light crept under the door
Like red efts in the sunset.

Two o's make an *oo* like holy book,
Shepherd's crook,
What the robbers took.

Take a sound like choo, add *s-e*,
last letter goes walking.
Heirloom lagoon, voodoo groove,
Caboose and the whole kaboodle.

Building an igloo out of vowels
Not for ballyhoo or boohoo or the old bugaboo
But in gratitude to the soil.
In remembrance of the swerving years.

      You don't think you know but you do.

Russian Wood

All happy families are like one another; each unhappy family is unhappy in its own way.
—Leo Tolstoy, *Anna Karenina*

So much isn't written because it's almost winter,
bare trees in the foreground,
scrape of light,
slant of wind.
And so when reading the opening of *Anna Karenina* to my love,
beautiful with her dog and a book in bed,
I understand there is nothing of logic to Tolstoy's setup,
only a way in for the rest.

Just like last week at the Silverbrook Cafe,
a band playing *The Tennessee Waltz* at our entrance,
Ramadan and Hanukah falling together,
full turnip moon backlighting the bar,
folks tripping across the lath of the dance floor,
not involved in a search for sequence
or god.

Right up till this moment of composition—
like a director forced by rain to shoot
the last shot first
the first shot last—
I have been someone else. Never thinking:

blue and yellow flowers blackened, yard white. Advent upon us,
Anna suspended beneath the wheels of a train,
a porter on the platform selling kvass.
How can birds be on the road
flashing tail white against standing dead trees?
How can a junco be small and in flight
but not leaves breathing?
How can there not be tenderness?

Inside Out

Yesterday we had a fight, call it an argument, really a disagreement.
I don't know what it was and then it sputtered out in the valley's muggy air.
The trouble had to do with words or maybe it was about the kind of life
one chooses to live. I sometimes choose to stand outside
to appreciate the inside which seems so threadbare
while I'm in it but then when I'm peeping into my own windows
there is this riot of color and life that abides with all its aroma
and noise until it stops.

Today I don't want it to stop. I want to rub your sleek back
with my aging hands like I did last night as if we were not in this
life of foolish misunderstandings but rather six rows back
watching a theatrical family on a life-like set, all the action
inside, fighting with each other over love. It made me cry.
I always cry in the theatre but not when I'm outside.

Four Years in Sandisfield

Buried in the glade cleared four springs ago,
remnants of my body will remain,
always, in the thrum of night.
This place of thick and thin trees was my dream.
What keeps is turning
a garden first and last,
lining trails with pine limbs,
voice rocketing into sky,
falling from mountains.
Great nodding rocking home of climax and anti-climax.

It's only human to sleep in a bed raised off the floor,
fuck on Sunday mornings, migrants streaming by,
step on the moon.

O magnificent osprey offering bloody fish to mate,
resonant chorus of Berkshire dusk,
I arrived with rage and delight
and when I go,
soon and soon enough,
I want to carry off the new love,
not save the angry furniture in this
house for sale.

Looking for the East Meadows

Bear right at potato fields
then left where swirling
dust swallows
all the days of your life.

Head toward a continent of dry corn
rustling in the language of a fifth season.
There will be sparrows in September
stillness gleaning the rows.

At the first fork straight.
At the T junction south.

If there's a box truck in the road,
its crib overflowing with kale,
back up. Slip in *Quintet for Piano and Winds*
from two centuries past.

Even though you think you're lost
don't fret over far off smoke or flocking white moths.
Ease into the tractor ruts.
Park by the pond where fill was gouged for the highway.

There will be accipiter hawks
and falcons gyring
the air and herons
splaying the mud flat.

Remember any day you see a kingfisher is a good day.

Remember life is most abundant at the edge.

That'll get you there.

Mid-Autumn's Eve

It happens in the dark,
reeling under the rotted eaves,
staring into blankness.
It happens carrying coffee grounds to the compost.
What an odd hour to be pressed by love.

It happens when the wind picks up
and unseen trees rustle
as contradiction takes the place
of stars in an insomniac sky.
Love, a thorn of light in otherwise blackest night.

Because of the gradualness that speaks of time,
as a thrush returns from death
after colliding with a window,
dawn washes out darkness with milk
like the faint blue cloud rising from your side of the bed.

For just one moment,
there, in a kind of clearing,
a season of inconsequence,
while sea smoke lifts from distant oceans
I stand in continuance,

a wolf tree,
feeding on the provender.

I Knew When I Saw This Place It Would Hold

When I saw your face
I became insistent.
Threw my heart over the fence.
      At times I've called it sabotage, suicide.
Dark as crows.
      I could be that dark.
Now I know it was none of that.
Certainly more than that.
I was born jumping.
It'll never stop.
I'm a horse.
Over and over, I throw my body over the fence.

Hairpin Turn

We placed a quarter in the vista viewer's slot
on the stateline overlook:
I saw mountains,
you saw heaven.
I saw rising meadow fog,
you saw animals hidden in thickets.
I saw the back of your skin, the rises and falls,
you saw teeth and hearts and banks of eyes among the clouds.

For I am the dead maple and you the smoke
and you are the bed and I am tired.
For I am the rapid ascent of love
and you are the body
and you the undeniable wind and I the dream catcher.
For I am fearful of darkness and light
and you are the opposite side of Earth.
And you a prayer, a blessing
and I the amen, the opening of the ark.

When the time ran out
and what we were looking for
when we were looking for love was done
we drove west.
All history fading in the vanished world.

II

I Can't Help Myself

I can't help starting with I.
It's what I often do.
I want to but can't remember

the spreading dogwood
wrapping our bricked row house
for a quarter of a century.
Perhaps it wasn't dogwood.
(Maggie says magnolia).
I don't recall blossoms.
I've squandered so much time
as it is.

I can't recall the angled look on your face
when we made love, for decades,
what we said over breakfast,
for decades.
You'd think I'd remember
some of that. It's startling
to conceive that I've consumed
the material of my life

though I've yet to braid the confluence
of falcons devouring
the brains of their prey,
(like butter, the falconer said),
with my father drizzling oil
over onion, chunks of black radish,
calf's brains,
his preferred way to end a day.

> I stuck a dogwood slip in dirt close by
> this four-sided clapboard house.
> It's thrived for five springs and five winters.
>
> Each morning before leaving
> he stares at it.
> He can't help himself.

In the Narrows

We sifted the contents of one plastic bag into another,
saving some of her for our missing brother.

Then we spilled her ashes into the sea,
into the atmosphere, onto our shoes,
and then we ate of her.

We fed our mother to the eels and crabs
and mermaids lurking behind the rocks along Shore Road
across from the traffic of the highway.

We fed our mother to the tidal strait
linking Upper & Lower New York Bay.

Her ashes spilled into the shallows,
clumping into the wholeness she lacked—
black headed gulls with darkened wingtips
shrieking above her form.

Coming together after seven years we fed
our mother's ashes to the wind blowing
five feet above the deep
while we leaned on the railing of the pier
watching waves carrying out to sea,
widening, then compressing,
returning her to Odessa.

We emptied mother out of a plastic bag—
only a name left, her journey just beginning—
but I see her as my children will see me
when I am powder mixed with earth

and as she prayed each Sabbath to three candle-flames,
for she was her father's daughter,
haltingly we recited the mourners' Kaddish

and then we ate of her
for we are our mother's sons.

Baby in the Boat

for Grandma Esther

Fleeing Kiev's bleeding limbs,
whispering beneath the full moon's terror:

Throw him over
before someone thinks to check
why a baby is wailing
in the middle of the night

Lake shadows rippling.
Mother biting her lips.

Eight of us want to live.
Throw him in
or I'll drown him myself

Wrestling off her youngest's pants
and there the open diaper pin
jabbing the fat flesh of her Abe
whose sobs heave to a whimpering halt;

then he sleeps and dreams
about the snow covering lawns in Buffalo
and his children, laughing,
burying themselves in it.

Meditation on a Dream Unrecalled

Loss has no effacement.
It flares with unremembered light.

On the artist's white canvas,
like an amputee's phantom pain,
absence suggests shape,

a boundary between two worlds:
the splash of phantasm and bludgeoning of the real.

      If I call up carefree night's geometry
with its colonies of dog-toothed violets in dappled dark,
it's the after-image of poems,
of trout lilies taking seven years to flower.

I'd swear there was the briefest image of blue space,
goats among fragmented stars.

And then while legs orbited silhouettes of elms,
goats vanished from an impossible sky—

        once it began
        it began ending—

only house painters left,
climbing ladders,
gessoing whispered stars.

Incident at the Baggage Carousel

Oh, I must keep my heart inviolate
Against the poison of your deadly hate
—Claude McKay, "The White House"

While waiting to claim my bags,
thinking I might kill someone,
I recognized the Indian by his angularity,
standing by the circular belt next
to another traveler, next to me.

A loosely taped cardboard box dropped
from the chute and Russell Means,
the tall braided man resembling my father
by the twitch of his fists,
moved in.

Under the terminals and tarmac of the Sunport,
named for the vast sky and great steel plates
refracting Albuquerque's heat,
lie patterned shards, arrowheads,
skull splinters of the valley people.

Russell barked *Excuse me*
to the blonde man who didn't hear
or was thinking of his bed
and so the son of shard potters
shoved the traveler aside...

Didn't you hear me?
What's wrong with you?
Grabbing the box,
the other stunned,
tottering.

Thousands of cities distant,
working his route along Newkirk Avenue
George felt a knife
pressed to his throat. Quickly his right
hand connected with chin

and the mugger's head smashed pavement—
comatose for a day then dying
in the municipal hospital. Then there was
the other man my father killed, years earlier,
without physical provocation, wielding a wrench.

Oglala-Sioux each day wake to bitterness,
spread honey on fry bread.
Old men dream of their fathers
hacked to death by Cossacks,
a hunk of black bread to staunch the bleeding.

People Next Door

After he broke my best friend Frankie Williams' glasses,
I slammed Ricky Richter in the solar plexus.
Then the Williams family drove upstate for the weekend.

That night, with news of Frankie's sudden death,
the building's mothers massed in our living room.
He was Catholic, the mirrors weren't covered.

I never could explain how I felt
at ten: Frankie, identical twin of Bobby, dead.
I knew their differences as I knew

the smell of roses rising from Mrs. Zinnie's garden,
the piano gleaming in her window, an American flag draped over the sill,
all the courtyard faced with red brick just blocks from the Hudson.

Even as I lacked understanding,
I meant to hurt no one.
Sometimes I've known what to do.

In Arroyo Seco where the setting sun
threaded through cholla like a raveling spool,
I told Filemon, the *viejo*,

if he ever laid a hand on my dog or raised his gun
I'd kill him
& he shut the door in my face.

In Flatbush the three sisters' bodiless heads out a window
gazed upon me double digging the earth.
Come summer they asked

why my blue & lavender hydrangeas
flourished while nothing grew in their unplanted dirt.
I offered, *You can't leave everything to God.*

In Bay Ridge false-faced Mrs. Cassidy complained when I tossed
a ball in my room & when I told her to shut up
my father forced me to apologize to that religious woman.

Still I haven't always known what to say
or the difference between right & wrong.
I shed no tears over Frankie's casket.

In South County curious neighbors wondered why sticks tied with rags
were stuck in my garden & when I shrugged
they departed downcast, sprigs of cilantro in hand.

The woman in the snow in Santa Fe,
her sisters helping her from the car, shower cap covering her bald head,
raincoat over her bathrobe open,

robe open too, as she stepped
carefully toward the dark end of the house.
I said nothing.

How romantic it seemed
coming west to the Four Corners
settling by the Animas, the Florida, Los Pinos;

like Henry Hudson sailing up the bay
before his crew mutineed, casting him overboard
to disappear in the river named after him.

I once saw Stanley telling Ollie that honesty is the best policy.
That wasn't square. If only Tom Paine were laid to rest with honor,
not simply thrown in a farm field, how different America would be.

Seven llamas stand in a Colorado meadow.
Brown-headed goats & greasy sheep shimmer on the county road.
In the next house I live in cardinals will again arrive late

& I'll wait to eat until they eat.
I want my neighbors to love me & I'll love them back.
We'll barbeque chicken, I'll play Muddy Waters loud

& we'll watch the birds flying back & forth between our yards,
the fences made of sycamore sticks or lilac.

Not Always Wishing for Truth

I don't know if we're in a garden
Or on a crowded avenue
　　　　　—Al Dubin, "I Only Have Eyes For You"

Wolves eat at night
and snakes smell with split tongues.
You bet I'm privileged, white American, never left
the corner, "4 hours short of benefits"
not a burden for the chosen.
But I can't see a thing in the sky.
Maybe millions of people go by.
That's how fresh it is.
From birth, apostatic,
first generation, carried like a stiff.
Bucky, laboring in mortuary storeroom,
described the bodies, *sacks of potatoes.*
Each morning, after showering, I'd fasten my bite suit.
Times so bad couldn't pick my own face out of a lineup.
We relocated to the Four Corners, presuming it
part of witness protection program.
Lately I've taken to visiting ruins, plentiful in the desert.
Could that have been a cardinal singing,
or The Flamingos?
There are none here.
Every spring my mother boxed the forbidden,
the treyf.
I'd walk it down to red-faced Mr. Keenan,
the super, on the ground floor.
I can barely say "church" without spitting up ash.
In the lobby, the Christmas children
caroled *down on your knees.*
Apologies to all my dead.
I'd rather see you than just hear voices.

What d'ya mean you're gone?
I just heard 'Shotgun*" on the oldies station.*
There's a dream about touch,
feel of one thumb, one tongue
pressing another. I had it then.
Now there's recognition.
The moon may be high.
If you don't remember dreams,
it may be you're entangled in someone else's.

In Reply To...

It's all right if this suffering goes on for years
—Robert Bly, "The Hawk in His Nest"

I'm not concocting metaphor
when I say a child was stolen from me
though even that's become dream now
or rather it never happened
because the child wasn't mine.

Ruined things are at the heart and the melody
will say it all. Still, why wouldn't it matter
how soft or loud the musicians play?
Yesterday you called today tomorrow.
Perhaps the argument is with yourself.

After the theme music fades, our cosmic
deejay replays irony mixed with tenderness
but irony won't be swallowed with ambiguity.
The sunflowers finally open but
their faces turn from the window.

I agree that not being forever cheerful is all right.
I hated how the boxwood shrouded the corner
of the house and while I hacked its roots with an axe,
my neighbor chained it, pulled it out with his tractor,
the mounded empty space a reminder of next things.

Yet the suffering, if it continues for years and there's nothing
to be done about it—that's okay?
Whether you believe Li Po drowned
attempting to embrace his reflection
it can't be all right if we never receive the love we want.

Sometimes it is our fault when things go wrong.
At the same time, who cares what others think.
You're just being provocative. If our action brings pain
it matters whether we regret it. Some scarlet tanagers
incubate cowbird eggs, others, male and female, abandon the nest.

Hunger

I help myself to material and immaterial,
No guard can shut me off, no law can prevent me
—Walt Whitman

Along the pink rock mesa
fronting two brown hills,
last spring's fledglings

attempt song.
I steal a flicker's flash of fire,
sun-glint on a kinglet's ruby crown.

I take all that I can.
Fear drives me to it.

Some birders place mist nets around yards,
catch incoming migrants,
hold blue-winged warblers to their mouths.

I gather feather and stone,
hang Jerusalem cricket
& clown beetle in the front window.

Dragging off all I can lug,
greed spurs me on.

From the newborn
desperate to talk,
I breathe evidence of fingers and toes,

and from their necks,
so goose-like they light the Rio Grande,
I rifle a message to my mother

about stars
that go on like numbers,
forever.

Then, running down the wash,
I thieve the blood wood of your heart.
Make it my own.

Without fear of consequence
I grab as much as I can hold.

Hunger makes me do it.

Saturday Night in Arroyo Seco, Abe's Bar & Grill

Shooting pool is like writing poetry:
pondering the uneven cloth,
gauging the corner's depth,
smacking the cue.

Straight pool the only game.
Not 8 ball.
Not rotation.
Straight poetry the only kind I know how to write.

On the high definition TV
two middleweights measure the angles,
pace the roped canvas,
batter each other.

My father whom I've been mourning lately,
not his death but rather his life,
won most of his bouts as a Bronx lightweight
but grandpa insisted he give up either boxing or my mother.

The locals in the smoky cantina
ignore me kissing
the 4 ball into the far side pocket.
Running the table,

I leave before the last round.

My New House

The Ute who lived here before us
stuck a salt lick behind a stump,
kept his quiver on the kitchen counter,
killed deer through the window.

When neighbors noticed his wife was gone
& the stench of rotting flesh grew stronger,
the sheriff came & dismantled the shed,
found a carcass of a half-butchered buck.

These first weeks a doe bounds down the ridge.
Sometimes she sleeps in front of the propane tank.
She won't leave when I shout.

Crossfire

El Camino Real slithers past casinos
in snakeweed, memorial crosses in Tesuque,
ravens in Truchas. Winter drifts
from mountains, covers rabbitbrush.

People say *I am who I am.*
Change is what's dropped in beggars' cups.

Everywhere you go in New Mexico
brown eyed susans,
Indian art in store windows,
painted ponies and money in pueblo dust.
Each curve alongside the Rio Grande
lizards scurry into talus.

Along the length of the Sangre de Cristos
on everyone's mind, in every paper
the lead story asking
What would you die for?

Shoppers caught outside Española
in the crossfire on Highway 285.
Workers in the no-fly zone departing Los Alamos,
mired in traffic, watching the sky.

Your lover drinking a six-pack, 5 shots of mezcal,
then running you over in afternoon rain
again and again. Jumping from the van
screaming *breathe, breathe.*

South of Peñasco a kingfisher flaps over Tutah Lake,
wind calm, day burned by sun.

Everywhere you are in America,
crow, vulture and sunflower.
All along the valleys, sphinx moths in geranium landscape.
Rain falling in the pines two days after rain.

After Driving Through El Duende, New Mexico

Duende is a struggle, not a thought
—Frederico García Lorca

Outside of Aztec I bumped a doe,
just a tap as I braked and veered.
She bounced off, folded up beneath the fender,
then stretched out young legs and rose
like a bridge table,
wobbling off into the cottonwoods.

Driving into moonrise in Española
I replayed the accident—
the deer no one owned
bounding along the shoulder.
When I finally got into bed
it was 90 degrees, sultry midnight.
I dreamed about obsidian,
its connection with aspen.
At dawn I awoke to a canyon towhee
threatened by its image,
scratching the front window.

This is not about seven points
or a circle of circumstance.
It's lightning arcing in Abiquiú,
deer at rest, hidden in high meadows,
ravens transecting smoke plumes rising in Taos.

A bird endangered.

Possible warnings of the day.

A Song for Clifford

There will always be birds beneath the window,
and racing lizards tunneling
crevices of slate.

There will always be mothers beckoning
children with the promise of weather:
Come out here...it's raining.

And they lunge
for the pavement, stand on tiptoe
in steady drizzle,
still amazed over lightning
strikes dreamed the night before.

There will always be those with halting
breath, calling Tuesday late into distant time
zones, fairly certain they won't see Sunday.

And the woman asking the clerk
for a book on trust:
My husband...It's getting so bad.

All the raveled days,
and at the finish:
Come out here...it's raining.

Always stems of shooting stars
and clods of earth.

A Song for Jack

We beat with our mallets of time and hope —Jack Handler

Dead flowers mass in the ravine,
all eyes on the leafy pile.
Earth moving no farther
no closer,

accepting always
the constant falling of dust
visible since we arrived,
swirling once we leave.

Most of life our eyes are shut.
Most of time we do not speak.
Yesterday, Jack
kept asking me the hour,

clutching his loving dogs,
through a hospital bed's metal bars.

~

Bumblebee unable to reach
nectar bites holes in tips
of columbine spurs.
One day it snows, the next

redwings gurgle first spring trill,
and the solitary sepals
and petals and stamens
dangling, burst.

~

A man is followed by the moon
marking the feast of lanterns.

He walks Blandford Road, gazes
round the curve with lightless eyes.

~

Jack died this morning.
Last week he asked
when I'd begun to write.
After the first time I made love I told him.

His skin kept changing color,
ravaged fingers
grabbing air. Then he slept,
woke and said

he dreamt of escape
but unsure from where. Perhaps
he pictured a barbed hook.

And leaving that.

Lucky to Have

In love with a woman
I thought I'd die with,
bumping down some wrong washboard road
in the drought stricken Rockies
even as snowfingers gloved San Juan peaks.

Across the dead meadow
and the crazy tract of double-wides,
a dark figure sunned on a boulder
craggy as an ark.
Distance like closeness can't be judged I've learned—
I was sure it was a bear.

Approaching by foot, twenty yards away,
yellow belly up, a sleeping rockchuck,
one more of Noah's lucky ones.
It was protected from all but the falcon
and must have figured that a chance worth taking,
basking there like a bum
with the glow still on.

I think of that rockchuck
as lilac sprays color
in riotous profusion
and how one time I stuck
my nose into Ponderosa pine
thirsty for its butterscotch
and when I inched my yellow cab
through Manhattan's sclerotic avenues
people scrambled into streets
hailing me.

I'd maneuver toward the curb
whether love awaited them or not,
hoping I could taxi them home.

Reentry

Returning to Earth was challenging for me
—Buzz Aldrin

On the surface of the Moon he had the thought he'd never die.
Now he realized he was better off
dead because of clowns counting

silver pieces in the marketplace.
And because of wooden houses topped
with bricked chimneys and the unaccustomed

light, the astronaut felt cornered,
for on Earth people are supposed to lead
their own lives; it was difficult for him

because of the fantastical insects and what the trees looked like,
standing every which way, taking no heed
of the constantly changing weather or loud voices on the street.

Doorsteps and thresholds confronted his every turn.
He was continually confused over sixes and nines
and the two meanings of "refuse"

and since he had seen the rising earth
and knew how slight it was—
here vast numbers of cemeteries bordering commerce,

the heaviness of home rooting him—
he recalled the lightness of that walk,
how all hunger vanished.

Still Life with Self-Portrait

Still life with half-finished business,

      expanding universe,   diminishing returns.

Self-portrait with sheet music for "All or Nothing at All"

        & exception

            like black crow with one white wing.

Still life with eyelash flames & Alexandria under water

        & excess

            like a tree before June drop straining

              under the weight of 2500 apples.

Self-portrait with lone sailboat

      heeling in the abandoned novel's harbor.

        Still life with cat asleep & cacti breathing

        in pre-Copernican universe.

Self-portrait on rotting docks washed by the come & go,

      speed on a gray surface,

        horseshoe crabs glinting in the wrack.

Still life with lit-up streets of New Haven, a display of witchery,

        & miniature plantains in Brooklyn markets.

          Self-portrait with imposed punishment in burnt umber,

            walking backward in Siberian sunlight.

Still life with high cheek-boned woman,

      nine hours six minutes of daylight,

        sizzle of garlic in scorched skillet.

Self-portrait in front row of bleachers,

　　　　at Three County Fair during demolition derby,

　　　　　　one fire only.

Stilled life with endocrine disruptors in town's water treatment plant

　　　　& little brown bats vanishing.

Self-portrait with unemployment check,

　　　　phone numbers scrawled on scrap,

　　　　　　boys sprawled on grandpa's lap.

　　　In the foreground, one too old to remember,

　　　　　　in the background those impudent enough to forget.

Still life,

　　　　　　not decorative vase & a bowl of rocks

　　　　　　　or oranges arranged on a plate

　　　but buried gleanings of an afternoon:

　　　　　this same face,

　　　　　　　starkness amid the roadside plowed snow.

It is still life after all,

self-portrait in the dark, deathlessly

       spinning a tale   secret even from the dreamer.

Still life with hive of paper wasps abuzz in a kitchen window

          migrating tarantulas by the Rio Grande,

        extraordinary

            visitation of owlets

            on St. Valentine's Day.

Self-portrait with alligator, with ibis, anhinga,

    first light in the Everglades.

Still life with creation's frenzy,

      skin,   scale,   feather,   leaf.

III

Doo Wop for Fidel

He wasn't yet a dictator
but a liberator
when he landed in Manhattan
with an entourage of 90 in the posh Shelburne Hotel
causing a disturbance
bop bop sh-wada
leaving behind bones and chicken feathers.

At first he threatened to pitch tents in Central Park,
then took peanuts, clothing, and beans to Harlem.
Fidel welcomed Krushchev to the Hotel Theresa on 125th Street,
crooning *there's a moon out tonight.*
Said to Malcolm *dance with whomever you want.*
Nehru hummed *The Wind.*
Nasser mumbled about Nubians
tending roses in Spanish Harlem,
then sang *Sh-Boom.*
Langston brought sugar cane still pink with blood.
doo-bop sh-bop

Fidel reclaimed 70,000 acres from U. S. companies,
half of it owned by United Fruit.
Malcolm said only a fisher would attack a porcupine.
Then, sending out a dedication to Earl and Sue,
all of them, a capella, on *My True Story,*
harmonizing *cry cry cry.*

Nose deep in perfumed hair,
dancing to *Angel Baby* with Marion Leone, thinking
how incredibly long this song by Rosie and the Originals lasted
and how thrilling & just that a rebel band
overthrew Eisenhower's gamblers & Batista's fascists
and on WNJR they were spinning a record called *Tshombe, Lumumba, Kasavubu.*
Life Could Be a Dream sweetheart
and listen, Marion,
Castro is addressing the General Assembly,
telling the whole world to dance
with the revolution,
but now it's 2007,
the old man
still top dog in Cuba,
quills stuck still in his white-tipped beard,
and Fidel is saying he wants to
stay just a little bit longer.

shoo be do bop ba da

The Flamingo's Tongue

"...the birds came down from the Northland during the autumn in numbers that were incredible, promising a continuation of the race forever...But these great armies...will be seen no more in our land, only the survivors of their broken ranks."
—D. G. Elliot, *Wildlife of North America* (1898)

Before Esteban Sevilla's concubine
who helped him sire 26 mulattos
informed him of the conspiracy to revolt,
and before the wife of the captain-general
told him that in her dream the house slaves,
serving coffee on the verandah,
slashed her throat,
and even as the civil authorities hesitated,
watching the wind dance of parrot rocking the cane flower,

the African thrown into the sugar house knew
that all that was visible in the early morning—
flocking yellowlegs, horizontal cane,
blood on the white-washed walls of the boiling charnel house —
would be gone within 3 generations.

Before the 4000 were shackled and the one from Congo
shoved through the doorless heat—
flesh chunks scattered like walnuts about the room—
from the swamp abuzz with hummingbird,
from the screw pine and razor grass,
a mongoose twittering, viper in its teeth,
came a cackling of flamingo,
Cuba darkened by the gabbling and wind
of the armies of heron.

There on the crooked floor before him:
knives for dinner
horizontal ladder
splintered humiliation
laughing Pancho Machete, plantation owner
screaming *boca abajo,*
his overseers stripping the man
on your stomach lashing him to the darkened wood
of *la escalera's* rungs
a double turn of rope around his loins

round his stretched back
binding the body immoveable
to the scourge of leather strips
their ends bound in wire.

In the distance the island's black triangle
of harbor and pilot boats shifting human cargo
No slaves, no sugar, no Cuba
so the accused would confess, then live or die.
They'd give up the names, any names it didn't matter,
for after the interrogation, the flogging,
the ladder was lifted
as mercenaries splattered with blood stood on other ladders
until *la escalera* was hung overnight from the ceiling
the man still fastened to it
blood staining the dark brown wood
like the blood of the flamingo after its tongue was cut
and served at Caligula's banquet.

Afterward
the one from Congo able to hear the croak of egret
able to see through the rung's spaces the wren
that lives only in that swamp
and mongoose no longer twittering
and through the next runged space
in the hurricane dance of October's wind
the white flower of the frangipani rocking.

Even the Dog Took on Vulnerability

*Too many speak of whip-poor-wills
as if they knew them.* "Against Whitman" —Ira Sadoff

How godly & sweet,
but if the leash snaps
as we cut across the road...

And the cranes,
how stately,
like a thicket of bald cypress
standing in shallow water,

but if the town fathers
in their piteous avarice
grant permission
to drain the marsh…

And the poets, too, how facile
when they write of thrushes
gaunt, arthritic, or especially *terrible.*
Don't believe them. It's only a flourish.

They're thinking of themselves,
of their parents' reflections in the mirror
before sleep overtakes them
and they dream in the dumb
contrivance of words.

Waxwings don't *perish* of old age.
They crash into power lines by Monte Vista,
fall in the hedgerows, picked off
by the dog running loose,
smother in the slick that oils the shallows.

People sicken in late winter,
ask for blessings from fly monks & high-heeled priests.
Better to travel the flyways
between scar tissue & survival.

Land in their own sweet Spring.

The Enticement of St. Anthony

When Saint Anthony stood on the banks
of the river Brenta and sermonized to the fish,
they shot up straight and listened.
He lured them with his pretty eyes,
soothed them with his halo of early spring,
season when death and birth equally tantalize:
choiring of bird then amphibian,
planting season succeeding anguish season,
nesting quickening with the surge of running sap.
Is it any wonder priests become pederasts?

Saint of swineherds and marriage,
saint of war and lost souls,
an anchorite spending his final days
under a branching walnut tree
in the company of his pet pig.

The real story is how Anthony struggled against temptation
even when baby Jesus was seen snuggling in his arms.
Satan hovered before him like a sparrow hawk
then appeared as a woman
imitating her acts of beguilement; Anthony of Padua,
"hammer of the heretics," stood fast.
Fearful Jews huddling in their ghetto were said to convert
after hearing of his ungodly resolve.

Patron of the poor, called forth in shipwrecks.
Saint of beaver, bass and black bear.
Saint of weeping eyes and unpredictable nature.
Saint for those neither sure nor ready—
the unrestrained, the yielding.
Saint for all those who resist.

One Day at the Junction

for Big Mike, Doc, Jack

When the cashiers got sloppy
it often led to small riots,
even fiery results,
but I ignored it when my crew drank
& every day at least 3 of them were tanked.
Sometimes I'd empty the bottles
I found in the filing cabinet
& maybe I did that day,
explaining why Al spent his break
at the Chesterfield Lounge.

Anyone could see he was polluted.
I had to punch his *social* into the computer.
One shark smelling blood ranted that
Al cheated him of $50.
I counted the tray, told the guy
the drawer was even
when he started rapping
the plexiglass with his finned umbrella.
After it cracked & the throng in the public area
joined in chanting *Rip-off Rip-off*
I pulled every cashier off the betting windows
& over the P. A. announced
there'd be no more action
till the guy left.

Horseplayers know a sure thing
& rarely falter in the stretch.
They flung him through the door in record time.
Days later fire broke out in Al's apartment.
He escaped, but his parents burned to death.
I was at the wake when a lawyer
dropped a business card on him, saying;
I'm sorry for your loss...You have a great case.

I didn't care if the cashiers drank.
You wouldn't either
if you spent 5 minutes there.

The Machine

Pete stroked the keyboard and daily doubles jumped out.
He slipped them through the window's slot.
No one was better.

Though his father, a lapsed Jew,
often called him a *mensch*,
Pete was brought up Catholic.

I worked with him when the pension was still 25 & 55.
On breaks the bettors,
relying on his speed,
treated him to drinks in Cheesey Pizza.

He was beery-eyed
when he asked what *mensch* meant.

I told him it was a high compliment.
Your dad saw you as a real man.

His slouch straightened,
his whole being changed,
for all along he thought
he was being called a fool.

1000 Islands

Last night in the pizzeria the label on the salad dressing ladle read
1000 Island &, even though it wasn't, I remembered that beautiful
late summer morning crossing the Verrazano-Narrows bridge leaving
New York City behind & arriving that evening in Chicago where for
the first time I was offered 1000 Island & I asked what it was then
ate it for 5 years running & afterwards we continued on to Madison,
Wisconsin & I was awhirl over the lakes & islands & lawns &
majestic houses & my brother found a rental with 2 other University
students & we stayed up late in what I thought of as my first bull
session talking sports & women & lust & one of the room-mates, a
skinny freckled red-headed science major working on a cure for
cancer, proclaimed he was repulsed by the thought of oral sex since a
woman's parts were so hideous & I, virginal & only partially white, or
so I thought since I was a Jew, argued bitterly for the first time in my
life &, thinking of Henry Miller's *Tropics* that I had secretly read, said
that the vagina was the most beautiful, mysterious, sacred part of
human anatomy. & he looked at me & said not a word

New Moon—Memorial for a Colleague

you think the moon is yours   for S.C.

I'll omit most of the contents

since my subject isn't the room

                with its elephant tusks & wall-eyed pike

            mounted above a glass case safeguarding

                        George Washington's collected writings

                        & the Babylonian Talmud,

but the new moon

                sandwiched in the imaginary line between our sun

      and earth—darkest hour even if less than a second—

& a reading that took place

                not this year but last

when to honor our dead friend

we read her chapbook,

thirty pages on despair, hope, cancer,

life after her husband walked out.

And by the way

                as the final poem, *Blown Roses,* opens

he wasn't among us in the Coolidge Presidential Library

                with its unhinged law-office door

                set against a roll-top desk

                close by a black-saddled mechanical horse

but his daughters were,

his sister, others who knew him

                though unlike how the new moon seems invisible—

                no ivory light cast from the dead star

                no copper aura enveloping the city—

                the light from his ex-wife's book reflected him

                refracting off colossal globed fixtures hanging

                from a wedding cake ceiling

as each of us—

                single, married, divorced, otherwise betrayed—

read in turn until the book was done,

reciting poems where his name wasn't mentioned

                even as it sounded from candelabra,

                echoed off a Dickensian chair,

                penetrated a Sioux headdress of eagle feathers,

                shook a collection of peace pipes & hatchet.

There were a handful of stage directions

mostly in the manner of *Exit Hamlet, Enter Ghost,*

only a few score notations,

I want him gone

no pianissimo, no forte,

no revelation of indiscretions except

I watched my lover take another woman's hand

only a scattered line here and there

I'm the woman feeling what a murderer must feel.

When Dexter Gordon and Freddie Hubbard Play
I'm a Fool to Want You

And when all that remained was dusk—
brown-eyed susans blackened,
finches warming in the darkened buckthorn—
and all my imperfections,
masquerades and handicaps, my near blindness,
when they weighed like the still faint
blinking stars, I turned to the tenor
for consolation, to the trumpet
for memory more precious than fact,
and the horns, throaty and coarse,
blew through absence and wind,
riffing above the scrub grass of jangled gravel,
sweeping to the hard-packed road
in an exhalation of spit,
blues up and down
in an exaltation of dust.

Dexter's tone like May in bird song,
like firefighters cradling heat imagers close,
searching for the children cringing in closets.

To save us when everything else is gone.

Talk of Sports and Youth Turns to Sex and Mourning

We count the times we've drowned to live
—Pam Uschuk

A colleague—I'd known him 15 minutes—
confides that his wife takes medication for depression
"and so we haven't had sex in years."
Next day Wayne the postman
explains that he and Mary are married
but "we don't sleep together."
Why tell me? Do I drip celibacy?
For that matter, what are they really saying?
No need to decide; irresponsibility naturally
derives from this style of narrative,
still, they must have decided long ago
to watch for cars exiting blind alleys.
They must believe God has already come.
They must reckon borrowed time needs to be repaid.

In the ragged daisies at driveway's edge
countless pollinators seek what's left
of "summer's honey breath," a last sweet taste
before frost withers every green
stalk, before winter's velvet horn drives
us into the hive's deep core.

We see it so often by this stage of life:
we fake the experience, grind our teeth,
build a barn to hold back the cascade of falling petals
while the cantaloupe sliced moon sails on—doesn't sail on.
For six weeks the blooms erupted
like circus clowns popping out a car
but don't bet on those last unopened
blossoms to flower.
As if we'd dare
glimpse a future to desire.

As if I could still imagine a November.

As if it were my business to know.

Kindling

Eyeing ice cleaving to highway walls like oysters to a shipwreck.
Waiting for soft wood to ignite hardwood
like heat lightning striking the mesa.
Peering at December's garden through circuitry of frost-stencilled windows.
Counting finches fox-trotting on husk-covered snow.
Following the wedge of scissoring geese heading to open water.
Scanning the backwoods for crow's nests snug in bowed pines
like callouses cobbled on a farmer's palms.

Thinking when I read your history in the tracery
of those crosshatched lines
how beautiful your crow's feet are—
tracks of filigree
etched in powder
by sparrow and dove claw.

Anonymous Love: Cecropia

If I could send you June's last breath in a country
of poetry: Main Street, 9PM, starry blight of defunct gas station marking
4 way stop and loops of chimney swifts chattering Florence into twilight.

If like a thrush I had two voice boxes
I'd sing you two hundred songs,
and as all the animals are younger than us

I'd swaddle thirteen wild turkey poults
in phlox leaf,
then speed them to your cove in the Sea of Cortez.

If I could fit a black bear yearling into the corner mailbox—
If I could tame one chippering bat, learn its tongue—
if I could post you the inflorescence of this life, spathe and spadix both—

Like silkmoths I have no mouth.
There's one week left to live.
Tent worms veil the wood.
All I do is search for you
among sugar maples.

      Any hour now, July—
and like the clown sweeping up his shadow
I wrap each minute of daylight lost.

As much as this is for old love

                                   we'll never have to lose it again
it's also for new love.
Sixty years it's taken to map this terrain of rise and slope;
everywhere I step in this tangled river valley
dinosaur footprints fossilized beneath my feet.

I plucked a swallow beak of lacewing and sawfly.

They flew off to you at first light.

Horse Story

One time Mr. Cooper cut his field
and brought the grass to Sheba
who'd already eaten
her morning hay & evening grain
but horses being what they are
she devoured the cut blades
and when we got home that night
we found her belly to the ground

       and just like T
       overdosing on junk—
       walking him back & forth in the small kitchen,
       the whole night,
       even slapping his face—

the vet said *make sure*
Sheba stays on her feet

       T & Sheba
       back and forth
       like Julius raging on his walker
       days before he died.

So we raised her,
walked her back and forth
till her withers tensed, rippled,
and she whinnied, bolted, then came round.

Before It Ended

with the chirr and flutter of an insect
fading against the cold
there was a woman I fell in love with at the movies.

When we kissed in the theatre
her dark eyes shined darker, desire blooming into her full face.
I remember how her long body trailed
like a trumpet vine across the bed,
and afterward, her worries over her son,
sitting up, telling of the daughter she lost in childbirth.

I had no idea what she thought of me, of us.

In the film, two lovers, foreigners in Manhattan,
become separated when the man is arrested
by immigration, locked in detention, then deported.

Late that night alone in the moonlit room,
how stark the crimson sumac fruit stood out
against the curbside's dry mullein and January sky,
holding by its woody stem through the worst of winter.

Birding Mount Auburn Cemetery, Cambridge

In the normalcy of this life,
how twins are born,
how rivers rise in early spring
and snakes hunt without arms or legs,
I fInd myself in a city I know only as a stranger,
searching lush cemetery grounds
for the stick nest of a horned owl.

Turning off Vesper Lane
in the shadow of early morning,
crossing Oxalis Path where it intersects Acacia,
facing a small circular marker next to a larger headstone,
the name "Robert Creeley" on one side,
a verse on the other

> *Look*
> *at*
> *the light*
> *of this*
> *hour*

a poet I'd heard once when I was young,
again when he was old,
laughing then as he read—
his one eye on the paper—
how difficult to get the last drop
to fall in the bowl
rather than on his thigh,

so normal and regular,
happening upon his moldering body,
both his eyes finally closed.

Carolina Wren

Like the roan horse standing at fence edge above the shoulder
he could see himself stepping from brittle snow to tillable earth.

Remarkable to believe
he could still beat the house
like when he turned the corner so sharply on his tricycle
tumbling down the open cellar's dozen steps of Vinnie's Grocery.

That he could even imagine in his state
        time on the horizontal
at his age
          pitch on the vertical

with all that sweeping his feet
swirling as the city did when his voice,
a ragged raven's wing, first opened.

And now his face tarnished
like silver dimes kept in the yellow cup
atop a dresser he wasn't sure why or when he'd acquired,
it appears that he could fall again.

That he could still weigh the possiblities
after living through wars of twelve American presidencies
that he might be roused at dawn her body in his arms
her hair in his teeth.

The fact that he would even imagine love
with all that sweeping his feet
whirling as it had when the O'Connor brothers
hoisted him from the darkened basement piled
with crates of blood orange and sweet onion

and even break into song like the southern wren
sweet william sweet heart
extend his range northward
until the hawk beak of winter cut him back
and then a step slower
he could start over.
Remarkable that he was so much like a horse like a bird.

The Extinction of the Black Rhino in Our Time, or
    Older Man Emerging from Flowers

I have not understood the world, and the world has not understood me
    —Pope Gregory XII

The sun is white and Earth so incomprehensible, so remarkably
obtuse, sunrays refract off muddied homes half in the river.
Until Nancy died, I hadn't grasped the significance when the flesh
of our feet turns mottled. Minutes after the hurricane
passed through, an inchworm yoyoed from the clothesline.
I heard a man being interviewed say *Integrity is an algorithm.*
Is that like saying human beings are resilient? That's so repetitive.
Besides, teratogenic products are widely available in every strip mall
and male frogs convert testosterone into estrogen, spawn
fertile eggs thanks to herbicide-generated enzymes. More news,
the tropopause continues to heat up. Rivers run brown with good dirt.

        But other times, say when night clangs its heavy gate
or when morning's another step up dream's lighthouse,
it is possible to understand this world. Except for Herbie,
every man I've known remains a man, every woman a woman,
every bull a bull and every cow a cow. Eleven thousand years
into the holocene, summer lasts longer. And still it ends
too soon but even as memory's rusted chain snaps
we continue to learn. Once, in the cemetery of the abstract
expressionists, a fireball streaked the sodden sky, painting
you into being. I knew then you were promised but not how
long it would take to find you. Even though magnetic north
is wildly unstable, sometimes I try recalling sheep in the middle
of a road, gaunt men wielding wide sticks, high-stepping
through the flock—what the air outside my car smelled like,
how loud their bleating shudder. Within my small circle,
each of us talks in our own way, just as sparrows' flight differs
from swallows'. We ask more than life will give.
Seeking the story of *my* life in others, what we look for,
through love and delusion, is ourselves.

Above this unlikely page hovers a fugitive from summer's finish—
a six legged fly with crossed translucent wings, bluish shell,
narrow reddish head and barrelled at the other end—
earthquake of jeweled flight, dazzle of deepest wonder.
Tomorrow will most likely find it dead. All I want is to recreate it
so you hear its buzzy song amid the plash of rain.

The Difference between Two Readings

Between the time I first climbed the Parabolic Dunes and the next
the world shifted but because blue-white Vega remains constant
I can make my way home. Because of the gap between who I think I am
and who I very well may be, the difference between two readings may resemble

the variance between three love affairs, a disparity between soundings
or why I devoured that novel when I didn't know better but now can't get past
the first chapter. It may be because of how Earth stumbles around our sun
that I impersonated the promise of myself and became who I am today

or perhaps I was more who I am then, than I am now. Back when I was thirty,
my child no taller than the dog, (both of them scratching at the cottage
    screen door), I was married
to a life. Twenty years later, realizing how much luck afforded me, walking
    arm in arm to the sandbar
and back chanting

Chequesett Neck Chequesett Neck, I managed to retrace the steps covered by
shifting sand and outrace the incoming tide. And today, even as the dunes
gather and disperse, sharing with another mysteries of April, finding
yellowlegs still congregating at the marsh, the vastness of my true identity—

beyond the interior fiction,
beyond the duress of illusion and the allure of the other,
or whether or not the novel's protagonist was switched at birth—
becomes clearer.

Because the river continues to crash from the spillway and the rush of
that river lights up the town and the snag jutting from distant rocks is
    clearly an eagle,
because there is wailing at the same time there is laughter I know,
am certain that the difference between two readings is day and night.

In Great Expectation

poetry costs money, cut it how you will, small or large
—Charles Dickens

Art is marginality, a critic says,
not about power or money,
but when we lived in Northern New Mexico,
people came from as far as Texas

to drink in Frank Morgan's alto.
Most didn't know about his time in San Quentin,
but swooned to his lower register,
mesmerized by blackness

in a land of Pueblo & Chicano.
Last Thanksgiving we passed through Mexican Water,
feasted on mutton stew.
Canyon de Chelly still has Navajo sheep farms

& homes built of rock
fitted into alcoves within sandstone walls.
Then, Acoma's Sky City, atop the enchanted mesa
where Governor Oñate severed one foot

from those responsible for killing his men,
those who had stolen the tribes' grain.
Then Gallup, which had no trees—
more like the Bronx.

Bars and pawnshops
with Jewish names run by Arabs;
Zimmerman's sold Tewa moccasins;
The Roundup, a place to down bourbon at 8AM.

Drab city in brown desert,
but Moab had pinnacles & spires,
balanced boulders & trees,
even a cow, tethered to a house off Main.

So much of what we saw was marginality,
you might have seen us
on the outskirts of town,
slipping through alleyways,

bending under arches.
Now in a square in New England
stands a statue of Sojourner Truth
who lived here in the boom years of silkworm and mulberry.

Bronze arms stretch out for American crows.
Legs grow from a draped granite pedestal.
Sojourner holds forth day and night: thirty years as a slave.
All right, no need to argue,

poetry is just a song, cut it how you will;
like *Scrapple from the Apple*
that Frank Morgan played as the sun set
one night in Taos under the Gorge Bridge.

NOTES

The last line of "Incident at the Baggage Carousel" leans heavily on "The New World" by Chana Bloch.

The epigraph from "A Song for Jack" is from Jack Handler's poem, "There Is No Turning Back."

Research for "The Flamingo's Tongue" utilized *Sugar Is Made with Blood: The Conspiracy of La Escalera* by Robert L. Paquette.

Quoted lines in "New Moon" are from the chapbook, *Blown Roses,* by Sue Case.

The epigraph from "Talk of Sports and Youth Turns to Sex and Mourning" is from Pam Uschuk's poem, "Meditations Beside Kootenai Creek."

"Anonymous Love: Cecropia" contains a quoted line from Leonard Cohen's "Tower of Song."

A Note from the Author

Great gratitude to my family, teachers, and friends who have helped in the making of this manuscript: Terence Malley, Bert, Maggie, Kate; Michael Waters and all the faculty and students I engaged with at New England College; my workshop partners over the years; Jay Udall; John Krumberger; Kevin Watson who put it all together; and especially Bill Root and Pam Uschuk.

Brooklyn born, currently living in Florence, Massachusetts, HOWARD FAERSTEIN has gone on to become first a bookmaker (OTB, not small press), then a wanderer of high deserts in New Mexico and SW Colorado, and now is one of America's legion of adjunct professors (teaching American Literature at Westfield State University) majoring in gardening, birding, and poetry. His poetry has appeared in numerous journals over the past four decades. A chapbook, *Play a Song on the Drums he said*, appeared in 1977. *No Sweat* and other plays have been workshopped and produced at The Westbeth Theatre in Manhattan.

Taking pictures, making pictures, is what inspires cover artist MATT PRIESTLEY. People, places, light, movement, emotion, performance; the public events of private lives.

It all began 20 years ago while travelling through the Far East: a taxi driver in Mumbai, an early morning on the banks of the Ganges, distant vistas of Himalayan peaks through Buddhist flags, all taken on the legendary Yashica T4 "point and shoot" 35mm camera. The journey, and, more importantly, the images, resulted in a huge life change. The day job was over. Matt is now an award-winning professional photographer based in the United Kingdom. The creativity, the infinite variety of people and situations, continue to make photography a passionate vocation.

Matt has hosted three personal exhibitions and collaborated on others. Social photography remains a focus of his output. As well as undertaking both personal and corporate commissions, he tutors other photographers and continually develops personal projects.

See more of his work at www.manchesterprpictures.com. Contact him at matt@mattpriestley.co.uk.

CPSIA information can be obtained at www.ICGtesting.com
Printed in the USA
BVOW080125210313

316055BV00002B/22/P